Beautiful
North Idaho

Beautiful
North Idaho

Text by Paul M. Lewis

Library of Congress Cataloging in Publication Data
Lewis, Paul M.
  Beautiful North Idaho
1. North Idaho—Description and travel—1951-
1. Title
ISBN 0-915796-94-5 (paper)
ISBN 0-915796-95-3 (hardbound)

First Printing March 1979

Published by Beautiful America Publishing Company
4720 S.W. Washington, Beaverton, Oregon 97005
Robert D. Shangle, Publisher

PHOTO CREDITS

CONTENTS

Beautiful America Publishing Company

The nation's foremost publisher of quality color photography.

CURRENT BOOKS

Alaska, Arizona, British Columbia, California, California Vol. II, California Missions, Colorado, Northern California, Northern California Vol. II, Georgia, Hawaii, Lewis & Clark Country, Michigan, Michigan Vol. II, Minnesota, Montana, Oregon, Oregon Vol. II, San Francisco, So. California, Texas, Utah, Washington, Washington Vol. II, Western Impressions.

FORTHCOMING BOOKS IN 1979

Massachusetts, Pennsylvania, Maryland, Wisconsin, Kentucky, Florida, Illinois, Ohio, Idaho, North Idaho, California Coast, Oregon Mountains, Nevada, New Mexico, Montana Vol. II, Rocky Mountains, North Carolina, South Carolina, Virginia, Oklahoma, Mississippi, Missouri.

1979 CALENDARS

Hawaii, Oregon, Colorado, California,
Michigan, Washington, Western America, Beautiful America.

Send for complete catalog, $1.00
Beautiful America Publishing Company
4720 S.W. Washington
Post Office Box 608
Beaverton, Oregon 97005

HIGH OVER PARADISE

The day was crisp but not bitter cold. Trailing cloud layers half-hid the upper reaches of hills around the lake and climbed the slopes of higher mountains in the background. The city of Coeur d'Alene glittered beautiful and white under its cover of snow, kept fresh by occasional flurries from the broken clouds moving through the sky. Large areas of the lake were frozen solid, as was much of the watery part of North Idaho.

Four men were out on the dock straining to ease a six-seat seaplane onto the ice from the end of the pier. After a few minutes of rocking the pontoons up and down and side-to-side, they gave a concentrated push and the little craft obligingly slid into the lake. One of the pushers was a visitor from a state where lake ice is not such a common phenomenon in winter, and he turned a little green when the ice shifted and cracked. The others in the party assured him that it would hold—''just adjusting to the weight, you see.''

Within a few seconds they were skimming across the bumpy ice. The plane, already warmed up while on the dock, seemed eager to get up into its natural element, as if the day, already past noon, would not last long enough for the trip at hand. Soon high above the cottony clouds scattered on the slopes, the plane banked and headed north toward the upper Panhandle counties. The Spokane River coiled away to the west, its route marked by the Post Falls Dam and the town of Post Falls.

North Idaho, by more-or-less common consent of those who live there, is a five-county area including, from south to north, Benewah, Shoshone, Kootenai, Bonner and Boundary counties. This slim corridor, also by unofficial consensus of North Idahoans, is the ''real'' Idaho, the ''business end'' of this pistol-shaped state. Here the rich natural gifts of Idaho seem to be composed by a nature bent on achieving unlimited variety in a mounatin, lake and river landscape. The airborne tourists in that winged rocking chair were treated to a succession of scenes remarkable for their gentle, although wintry, beauty. The dense stands of evergreens contrasted sharply with a winter dress of white on the mountain slopes, and the lakes and waterways glittered with a metallic sheet of ice.

The picture is still very close to what it was when the Indian tribes were the only human participants in the drama. Pristine, close-packed forests covered the mountains up to the crests. If a North Idaho resident from 200 years in the past were able to join the flight, the major differences he would notice would be the occasional clusters of buildings at lake edges and on river banks, and the bigger towns sitting snugly along the woodsy drapery of the mountain folds. In this winter season he would see occasional long, white threads, some thick, some thin, stretching through the mountains from north to south and east to west: roads, linking the towns and buildings together without marring the land in any overpowering way.

The plane's occupants strained to get a concentrated look at a giant starfish whose many arms seemed to be wrapped in evergreen woolens. This was Hayden Lake, just north of Coeur d'Alene Lake. It was pointed out (rather unnecessarily) to the Idaho visitor as a lake of surpassing beauty. Its many deep bays not only give it an elegant profile; they add up to a shoreline far more extensive than is usually allotted to small lakes. Coming up under the port side were two more in the parade of lacustrine masterpieces: Twin Lakes and Spirit Lake, calm and perfect in their forest and mountain settings. Spirit Lake, the town, was there, too, and Twin Lakes Village. Soon Pend Oreille River passed under the wing and the town of Priest Lake could be seen over on the west. Big Pend Oreille Lake spread out like a giant white-and-dark-blue carpet beyond the ridge to the east, but the travelers would visit that lake a little later on their return trip along the east side of North Idaho. Ahead were the southern reaches of the Selkirk Mountains, a beautiful and lofty range that Bonner County shares with Boundary. The Selkirks' beauty is created in part by the deep cirques or basins on their rugged slopes. As the plane skimmed over the crests, the men could see the frozen, white surfaces of the small mountain lakes which have filled these glacially carved bowls.

Priest Lake was the next attraction for the *voyageurs*, a long, narrow gem of a lake that glitters in the northwest corner of Idaho. The wild terrain below was possessed of white and green loveliness that momentarily imposed an almost-reverent silence on the group. To the right of the aircraft the Selkirk Crest reached up with menacing sharpness. As the plane turned south on the east side of the Selkirks, the thin finger of Upper Priest Lake appeared in the northwest, its frozen surface throwing off a white radiance that the slanting rays of the midafternoon sun seemed to set ablaze. Invisible under the thick forest covering between Upper and Lower Priest was the narrow channel of water connecting the two lakes, built by nature and called by men "The Thorofare."

"Look! There's Chimney Rock!" someone exclaimed as they flew past the Selkirk crest and over the eastern slopes. Right there on top of a high peak rose a perfectly straight column of rock looking something like an enormous tower on the face of the mountain. The sun was low in the sky and its golden light lit up a narrow band of mountain top, tower and all, in a fiery brilliance quite overwhelming to the quartet of rubberneckers.

To the left of the aircraft as it headed south lay the massive bulk of the Cabinet Mountains, still lonely and mysterious even though signs of civilization could be seen on their edges. The tracks of the Burlington Northern defined their perimeter like a giant hem. A few forest service roads probe the isolation of the Cabinets, which stretch east into Montana, but a ground-level trip through the dense forest must wait for summertime when the roads are open.

Necks were stretched for the first glimpse of the northern shore of Pend Oreille Lake, coming up ahead of the plane's nose. Sandpoint, a big town for this neck of the woods, sailed past under the right wing, moored by its two bridges coming up from the south. The railroad and highway spans walked over the water just before the big lake narrowed to become the river that drains it to the west. Sandpoint looked fat and contented in its low nest between the waters and the woods.

As they passed over the bulbous north end of Pend Oreille Lake the men could see some of the small communities along the shore, towns like Kootenai, Ponderay, Sunnyside, and Hope, looking like neat little buttons on the skirts of the forested mountains. Over on the east

8

(Preceding page) Heavy plumes of bear grass bend on a hillside overlooking Lake Pend Oreille, near Clark Fork.

(Opposite) Bonner County's winter couldn't quite stop this waterfall near Castle Rock.

(Right) "Showy hygrophorus" seems an apt name for this colorful fungus, found where the earth is moist.

(Below) The St. Joe River is revered for its placid beauty.

(Following pages) The irregular shape of Lake Coeur d'Alene gives it miles of unspoiled shoreline.

(Third following page) Colorful wildflowers highlight this meadow on Marble Creek, in the St. Joe National Forest.

(Preceding page, above) Brilliant colors indicate that autumn is on its way in this view of Clifty and Black Mountain from Katka Face, in the Cabinet Range.

(Preceding page, below) Silt deposited over many years by the St. Joe River has formed levees far into the waters of Lake Coeur d'Alene.

(Left) A peaceful backwater of Pend Oreille Lake captures a perfect reflection of trees and clouds on an autumn day.

(Following page) Chimney Rock, ''the lightning rod of North Idaho,'' offers an irresistible challenge to rock climbers.

(Second following page, above) Slanting afternoon sunbeams touch this golden stubblefield with light and shadow, in the Plummer area on Highway 95.

(Second following page, below) Bear grass covers this hillside on Lunch Peak, in the Kaniksu National Forest.

(Third following page) The Thorofare, connecting Upper and Lower Priest Lakes, meanders gently between pine-shaded banks.

(Preceding page, above) Wildflowers brighten a meadow along this quiet stretch of North Idaho's Coeur d'Alene River.

(Preceding page, below) Two small islands break the waters of Hayden Lake, and pines prove their tenacity by grabbing a toehold even on the smaller one.

(Left) "Vermilion Hygrophorus," modest of stature but brightly colored, is another of North Idaho's native fungi.

(Below) Broken clouds hang low over the Kootenai River and Valley in this view from Katka Mountain.

(Following page) The rugged landscape of Boundary County offers small lakes of unusual beauty, like Roman Nose, in the Selkirks.

(Second following page) Golden birches of autumn scatter the Pend Oreille River banks with a rustling layer of leaves.

the Clark Fork Estuary resembled a watery maze, with the river picking its way among numerous islands before committing its waters to the big lake. The town of Clark Fork, snuggled up against the hills back of the river's mouth, was more a promise than a reality as the airborne snoopers struggled to catch a glimpse of it.

The small craft flew low over the main body of Pend Oreille Lake, which seemed even more vast because of the proximity. The huge, glacier-carved basin contains one of the largest freshwater lakes on the continent. Its closeness under the airplane managed to make everybody feel very fragile and inconsequential, which is also a common feeling on Pend Oreille when one of its famous storms abruptly appears, goading the surface into a roiling, foaming mass of angry waves.

Pend Oreille is different from the other lakes, big and little, in North Idaho. And not only because of its lateral extent. It's a good deal deeper than the others, for one thing. Coeur d'Alene, the next biggest lake, is quite shallow in comparison, in the 200-300-foot range. Pend Oreille is more a sea than a lake. Its maximum depth has been measured at 1,152 feet.

But statistics were not on the minds of the high fliers in the low-flying seaplane. As they passed over the western shoreline they pointed out for the benefit of the visitor among them some of the landmarks on the eastern shore, sometimes with tales of adventures, real or imagined, connected with the particular spots. There was Deadman Point, Indian Point, Windy Point, Kilroy Bay, Pine Cove, Granite Point, and so on. While they were thus engrossed, one of the most knowledgeable, with commendable care for detail, observed that not far to the west was little Cocolalla Lake, which could not be seen because of the intervening ridges. But Cocolalla is right next to north-south US 95, so it is easy to visit for anyone who wants to see it or fish in it.

Whiskey Rock, above the "lobe" of the ear-shaped lake, was ostensibly named for the miraculous salvation of one fortunate boatman who had wrecked his vessel upon the rock one freezing day. He had only preserved himself from turning into a very dead icicle during the night by consuming a liberal amount of hard stuff until he was rescued. It made a good story. Somewhat more factual was the startling (to the visitor, at least) revelation of the giant Kamloops trout that dominate the lake waters. The Kamloops at times weighs in at 30-plus pounds. He gets that way by feasting on the smaller Kokanee (a landlocked sockeye salmon) and other species that also thrive in Pend Oreille.

The glacier that scoured out the big lake's basin cut such steep cliffs along much of the shoreline that lake access, except for the comparatively level north shore, is limited to selected spots. Garfield Bay, on the west side, is a popular access point. From the seaplane it appeared perfectly rectangular, with resort lodges and marinas clustered around it. At the lake head in the southern tip the pilot dipped a wing at Bayview, the premier resort town on the lake, its importance owing largely to its accessibility to vacationers from Spokane. The presence of Bayview, Garfield Bay, and a few minor landings around the "pendant" portion

(Preceding page, above) Geese paddle in the chill waters of Oden Bay, below the Schweitzer Ski Area, where the ice has not yet closed in.

(Preceding page, below) Lake Elsie is high in the rugged Coeur d'Alene mining region.

of Pend Oreille reinforced rather than diminished the wild, rugged appearance of the lake and the awesome cliffs that contain it. From a low-flying plane, especially, the scene stirs up a feeling of wonder tinged with fear when one is confronted with such a prodigious show of natural power. The steep sides of the basin plunge into a deep, deep pool about 44 miles in length (from Buttonhook Bay to Dover). Because this particular flyover took place in the winter, the lake ice, gleaming dull white, may have added to the feeling of some on the plane that they were in the presence of something elemental. Large patches of open water, looking like great black holes in the surface, seemed to impose another layer of mystery. The mighty phenomenon of Pend Oreille Lake, almost incomprehensible in human emotional terms, left at least one of the fearless fliers a little shaken as he looked back now on the retreating shoreline of Buttonhook Bay and Farragut State Park at the head of the lake.

The late afternoon light was still good as the plane headed back toward Coeur d'Alene Lake, flying over level ground that represented an extension of the Purcell Trench, the glacial gouge that comes out of British Columbia into Idaho and is partly occupied by the monumental lake just left behind. To the west was Rathdrum Prairie, a morainal fill of great fertility, where seed grasses are grown on a commercial scale. And underneath it all was the Idaho Aquifer, Pend Oreille Lake water that filters through the gravel of the moraine and is drawn up for irrigation.

Before very long the aerial excursionists were within sight of Coeur d'Alene, the city and the lake, and one of the party suggested that the pilot fly up to the head of the lake and back, to give everyone a really good view of what is considered one of the five most beautiful lakes in the world. With a little imagination one can discern on a map that the entire lake forms a scraggly "E" shape, with the top leg at the north end, the bottom leg at the head of the lake, and the middle leg suggested by the bulge of Carlin Bay.

Passing over the top of the "E," everyone looked east into Wolf Lodge Bay with appreciation for the fjord-like contours of the big northern arm and especially of the two small bays on the north and south of Wolf Lodge. Beauty Bay, the southern one, is celebrated the world over for that quality. It has been photographed zillions of times from the scenic road high up on one of the tree-covered hills that take a steep plunge into its waters. Its pure waters are free of ice a large part of the year, and much has been written about the ever-shifting color and texture of its surface caused by sun, winds and clouds. Among the creatures who favor it are eagles, and other birds of prey which gather there during the salmon run.

The plane moved up the lake, passing over some open water, profoundly blue in contrast with the ice. The sight brought some expressions of mild surprise from the North Idahoans. "Well, after all, our climate's getting warmer," someone offered. And in truth, this appears to be the case. North Idaho's ice needs were once amply supplied by ice plants located on some of the smaller lakes, like Cocolalla. But the weather here has always been moderated by

(Following page, above) Some photographers claim that the still waters of the "shadowy St. Joe" provide reflections that look more realistic than the real thing.
(Following page, below) Sunset deepens shadows and brings color to the still surface of Lake Coeur d'Alene at Harrison.

Pacific winds and protecting mountain systems. It is considerably milder than that of eastern Washington (the annual mean temperature in places like Sandpoint, Kellogg, and Coeur d'Alene is close to 50 degrees Fahrenheit.)

The best way to see Coeur d'Alene Lake during an aerial reconnaissance is to have at least 100 eyes and several heads that swivel in all directions. Bay follows upon bay, each one very different from any other. On this occasion, as the aircraft made for the lake's head, the promontories and the bays gave everyone a rapidly changing impression of the lake's profile. In quick succession Squaw Bay was pointed out, then Arrow Point, Echo Bay, Driftwood Point, Mica Bay, McDonald Point, Carlin Bay, and so on. Powderhorn Bay, near the lake head, made no bones about how it got that name.

The Coeur d'Alene River showed up nearby. It entered the lake from the east, accompanied by a string of small lakes whose temporary winter coat of white gave promise of spring and summertime splendor. The river, like the St. Joe, its famous peer a few miles south, creates its own banks where it feeds into the big lake. The river's course was clearly marked by vegetation long after it should have merged into the anonymity of the lake waters. On a bulbous promontory by the big lake, where the river entered it, sat the hillside town of Harrison, about the same size as it was when it began in 1891. In the early days it had vied with Coeur d'Alene for business supremacy. Both towns used to have reputations as wild weekend haunts for miners and loggers. Harrison has long since dropped out of the economic race, but it is still emblematic of the good life to a corps of loyal residents who like their town just as it is.

As the seaplane banked for the return trip to Coeur d'Alene, the "shadowy" St. Joe pulled onto center stage below. Glittery rather than shadowy on this day, it was no less impressive as one of North Idaho's exceptional waterways, its slow, sinuous course through broad, fertile meadows still going on as usual under its temporary outer garment. The levees piled up by the river as it flowed into the head of Coeur d'Alene Lake looked something like two gracefully curving, parallel railroad tracks. One of the banks appeared to have worn away well along into the lake, a latter-day phenomenon, caused by the force of water pushed by motorboat wakes.

The hard-working little seaplane turned north, pontoons and all, and headed home. By the time it reached the dock at Coeur d'Alene the elapsed time of the trip would still be under two hours. The Idaho visitor sat musing on this as he looked out of the starboard window at the complicated lake shoreline and the hills beyond. The sun was dropping over the horizon, and the lowering light began to blur the outlines of the distant landscape. It had been an exciting two-hour odyssey, even for the long-time North Idahoans.

People who live in this land, even for a very long time, find it impossible to become jaded about the Panhandle country. The visitor sensed that this close affection for their land was rooted in more than its sumptuous physical spectaculars. Life here had in the past molded a separate, very independent, very enterprising type of individual and was still doing so. For

(Preceding page) The thin ribbon of Copper Falls plummets into a tiny pool at the base of its rocky escarpment in Boundary County.

30

many of these people, to live in some other place would be to imitate that well-known fish out of water.

Still absorbed in these thoughts, the visitor hardly noticed the smooth landing on the ice of the lake. The plane was gliding up to the dock before he realized the bird's-eye view of this magnificent land was over. Already it seemed like a fantasy. He was afraid the lakes and the mountains and the rivers in all their kaleidoscopic combinations would vanish in a twinkling, and that all he had seen would be nothing more than a sumptuous dream created by some overworked sub-level of his mind. But it was all still here: the serene blue sky, the gold-edged clouds trailing through it, the lake and the land, and his companions on the flight. They all climbed down from the plane and watched from the dock as the pilot maneuvered it closer in. It had been for everybody an afternoon filled with visual pleasures, and for one of them at the very least an unforgettable moment to be treasured his whole life long.

(Following pages) A springtime breeze ruffles the broad expanse of Pend Oreille Lake.

COEUR D'ALENE AND ALL THAT

The cities of North Idaho are not just *places.* They are living, pulsing parts of the fabric of the land. They have personalities, all different, shaped during the years of their involvement in the history and growth of a raw land that has always offered great rewards to those with the ambition to look for them and the guts to live by their efforts and wits. All of the towns in the Panhandle where people have collected and set up housekeeping have their separate identities, yet the traditions and roles of each in the continuing history of the region have linked all together, from mere hamlet to the flagship community of the region, Coeur d'Alene itself.

Heart of an awl. The name, Coeur d'Alene—city, lake, and river—is a legacy of French Canadian trappers who may have thought they were giving a back-handed compliment to a small Indian tribe of the region with whom they traded and who were at least as sharp as they in the trading business. So the name: the Coeur d'Alenes or Pointed Hearts, Heart of an awl.

The city of Coeur d'Alene began life as a military fort in 1878, courtesy of William Tecumseh Sherman, the general of Civil War fame. Sherman visited the lake when it was a stop on the Mullan Trail, the old military road from Fort Benton, Montana, to Walla Walla, Washington. He did a little sightseeing, enjoyed the scenery, and recommended the spot as a location for a military post. For a while the ''town'' was just the fort and a few civilians who came along to supply the needs of the soldiers stationed there. Two years later the first steamboat, the *Amelia Wheaton,* was built by C. P. Sorenson under contract to the government. Sorenson also became the captain of this initial lake steamer and later gained fame as the ''father of Coeur d'Alene boating'' by building many of a long line of lake steamers in partnership with P.W. Johnson, who arrived in 1889. Sorenson is also credited with naming most of the bays and points on Coeur d'Alene Lake.

The neophyte town didn't really start to expand until a gold prospector, one A. J. Prichard, made a strike in the Coeur d'Alenes in 1881, held his tongue until 1883, then finally blabbed about it in Spokane. The rest is history, as they say. Coeur d'Alene became a sort of way station on the route to the mines and soon began building buildings more permanent than tents. Hotels, saloons, dance halls, bawdy houses—anything to make a buck from the flood of miners—sprang up in record time as the nucleus of a rough, new town. Two more steamers were built in 1883-84 to cash in on the transporting of miners and supplies up the Coeur d'Alene River to the head of navigation. More boats were built in the later eighties to take care of the rush of mining business.

When the railroads were built, with a branch line into Coeur d'Alene, lake excursions became popular on the weekends, with crowds from Spokane arriving constantly. The steamers took them across the lake and up the Coeur d'Alene, St. Joe or St. Maries rivers. The excursion business proved a great boost to the economy of the new city, which by the era of the nineties had all the accoutrements of civilization a town was expected to have in those days.

Coeur d'Alene had a second birth with the coming of big-time logging toward the end of the century. The white pine forests of the St. Maries Valley and the Coeur d'Alenes supplied the raw material, floated down the St. Joe and Coeur d'Alene rivers and kept from jamming by "river pigs," who endured a harsh existence in those early log drives. Coeur d'Alene Lake became a huge millpond feeding the lumber mills at Coeur d'Alene and Harrison.

The St. Joe, Coeur d'Alene, and St. Maries rivers all are feeder streams for Coeur d'Alene Lake. The latter river joins the St. Joe at the town of St. Maries, the Benewah County seat. St. Maries figured prominently in the Coeur d'Alene region's early-day logging boom and is still an important lumber town. The town sprawls over hills in white pine forest a few miles east of the lake head. These waterways have been an inseparable part of the history and economic activity of the area ever since. Gold was discovered in the rocks of the Coeur d'Alenes, and then "gold" in the form of white pine stands began to be harvested from the rugged slopes around the St. Maries Valley. The rivers have always been transportation routes, at one time for miners on their way to the ore deposits, then later for massive log drives. The exceptional charm of the Coeur d'Alene and St. Joe and the beauty of the meadowlands lining the course of the lower rivers have attracted admiring visitors since Indian times.

Because of the mining activity in the hills around it, the Coeur d'Alene had become more and more polluted until very recent times. In the words of one disheartened commentator, it had gone from a deep, crystal-clear stream, with cottonwoods and beeches arching over its banks and lush grasslands running back into the hills, to a waterway fouled with slag. But in the past two decades environmental controls installed by mine operators are bringing the South Fork of the Coeur d'Alene back to its former glory. Mine tailings are confined to settling basins and pumped back underground; one big mine (the Bunker Hill) has constructed a secondary treatment system to remove heavy metals from processing-plant effluents.

Back around the middle of the nineteenth century, when the river was a true wilderness, a graceful Renaissance-style church was built near the present-day Cataldo. This was the Mission of the Sacred Heart Of Jesus, first erected as a log structure on the St. Joe a few years before in 1842, then abandoned because of floods. The Old Mission, as it came to be called over the years, is protected now as a historical monument, the oldest building in Idaho. It was constructed by Coeur d'Alene Indians under the guidance of the Jesuit priests Father Pierre Jean deSmet, who selected the site, and Father Anthony Ravalli.

To the south of the Coeur d'Alene river is the other major feeder stream for the lake.

(Following page, above) Reflections in the waters of the peaceful St. Joe River are especially striking in autumn.
(Following page, below) Spectacular clouds mount in the sky over Rathdrum Prairie, north of Post Falls.

The "slow St. Joe" has become legendary in the relatively short time since it has figured in the affairs of western civilization. Its abrupt change of personality from the head of navigation, normally at the town of St. Joe, downriver 30 miles to the head of the lake, has captured the imaginations not only of longtime North Idahoans, but of the many visitors drawn to its wild and serene beauty from all over the world. North Idahoans are fond of pointing out that it is the highest navigable river in the world (2,198 feet at head of navigation.)

The "shadowy St. Joe" is another affectionate descriptive for this river of fond memory. There seems hardly a breath of current in its green depths as it wanders placidly through a wide and fertile green valley. The cottonwoods and willows that line its banks are reproduced to startling perfection by its smooth-as-glass surface. Photographers of the river's banks have a hard time deciding which part of their pictures is the reality and which the reflection. Some claim that the deep river waters give the scene a surreal or super-real dimension.

Even though the St. Joe and St. Maries river valleys have been settled since late in the last century they have been treated kindly by civilization and remain essentially the transcendently beautiful environments they were when the Indians were the total human population. Wildlife is still plentiful. Raptors such as ospreys, for example, build their nests along the river banks. The towns of St. Joe and Ferrell, across the river from each other, had reputations as wild and rough places, especially on weekends when the loggers stopped swinging at trees and started on each other. At the turn of the century, when the Milwaukie Railroad was being pushed through the Bitterroots along the St. Joe Valley, the railroad construction crews came out of their tunnels on Saturday night to add to the mayhem. A road, paved in some stretches, wanders along the banks of the river and reaches up into the hills, to the charming little mountain towns of Calder and Avery, remembrances of things past along the whitewater part of the St. Joe.

One of the facts of life is that beauty has its dark side. Settlers in the St. Joe Valley from the earliest days to the present have found that out. The hideous truth is that the gorgeous river is not always a model of perfect behavior. It floods. In the past, the rampaging river, swollen by springtime freshets, chased the "Old Mission" to higher ground on the Coeur d'Alene River and forced Captain Mullan to relocate his military road. The Swiss settlers who first located on the lush green meadows of the St. Joe stuck it out and have remained a stable community in the valley ever since. Relatively minor things like floods could not uproot them from the rich bottomlands that were giving them a comfortable livelihood. Nor, to put it in non-practical terms, could the floods make them leave a valley whose gentle beauty defies comparison with any other place on earth.

Coeur d'Alene has kept on growing at a modest pace all through this century. Lumber and mining are no longer its only concerns, or even its major ones. The idyllic lake setting and surrounding hills have helped to make the community one of the nation's premier summer resorts. The climate, rarely hitting the extreme ranges, has helped bring it to the notice of more and more vacationers and people looking for the right location for a permanent

(Preceding page) The deep-blue waters of Roman Nose Lake provide the perfect mirror for the Selkirk Mountains' rocky ruggedness.

home. The predominant colors are blue and green: the brilliant blue of the lake and the soft green of the lawns and tree-lined streets in the residential areas. The town rises gently from the lake shores, nestled snugly around its best-known landmark, Tubbs Hill, a tree-covered eminence almost totally preserved by the city as a wild area.

The heritage of the past is still one of the engines that pulls Coeur d' Alene ahead. Many of the movers and the shakers of earlier decades are still around and still very active. They are the people of great initiative and talent who not only enjoy the good life but find real pleasure in putting their backs and minds into efforts for the good of the community. The civilization of North Idaho was built by sweat and perseverance; the tradition, passed on to the present day, is money in the bank for Coeur d'Alene and other Panhandle towns.

A historical connection of major significance in the life of Coeur d'Alene is Fort Sherman, remembered nowadays in the various artifacts perserved from the time when it was an active military post. People in these parts have a huge affection for the fort, sold by the government in 1902, and have turned the grounds into a city park. A small museum (the old fort's powder magazine) houses post memorabilia, including the Army order establishing it, uniforms of the period, officers' swords, and Indian costumes, tools, and cooking utensils. As an example of the care for the past typical of Coeur d'Alene, some of the officers' homes and other buildings from the fort have been preserved and restored. They are being put to various uses by North Idaho College, a two-year community college whose campus occupies a sizeable share of the old fort grounds.

Many Coeur d'Alene people have summer and weekend homes across the lake on the near shores and in the bays. The wild shores to the west and south have practically no roads into the hinterlands back to Mica Peak. So the water's edge is dotted with moorages from whence the trip to town is an easy ride by power-driven boats or even sailing craft. Coeur d'Alene residents do not consider their lake a barrier in any sense; in this rugged terrain it's a handy highway with no detours. The lake rarely freezes over, but when it does, snowmobiles run over the surface, and even sailing skiffs fitted with runners go careening along, all at a fast clip. The sail is king of Coeur d'Alene in the summer, when regattas make this superb lake even more gorgeous, if that were possible, by the massed presence of graceful craft and brilliantly colored canvas.

The Coeur d'Alene country would certainly seem to be in for some rapid growth in the next decade and beyond. It has just about everything anybody could want as a place to put down stakes. There's nothing namby-pamby about it, from the weather and the setting to the people who live there. It has four distinct seasons, from crisp winters to delightfully gentle springs, to delicious, warm summers, to Indian-summer autumns with all their wonderful colors, aromas, and soft light on the mountains and lakes. If the town and the lake and the surrounding region can grow without altering in any far-reaching way the charm of the land and the free spirit of the people then Coeur d'Alene will become a model for what people can do when they're made of good stuff.

(Following page) Striking in its deep blueness, Little Harrison sparkles like a gem in the pine-clad mountains.

(Preceding page) The view from Mineral Ridge encompasses Beauty Bay and much of the Wolf Lodge Arm of Coeur d'Alene Lake.

(Opposite) Lake Darling is one of the high-country lakes in Bonner County.

(Right) The ubiquitous Indian Paintbrush brightens landscapes in North Idaho.

(Below) Wintertime brings snows to the banks of Bugle Creek, in Bonner County.

(Following pages) Evening's stillness settles over Priest Lake.

(Third following page) Sunlight barely reaches the floor of this grove of old-growth cedars in Bonner County.

(Preceding page, above) This is the appearance of the Clark Fork River near the North Idaho town of the same name.

(Preceding page, below) Autumn brings hues of gold and russet to the ranches in Bonner County.

(Left) A massive pine tree frames Beauty Bay on Lake Coeur d'Alene as the camera looks across Wolf Lodge Arm and the Interstate 90 bridge into Blue Creek Bay.

(Following page) Pine trees in the Schweitzer Basin Ski area assume grotesque shapes under their burdens of snow.

(Second following page, above) Beauty Creek drains a wooded glen near Lake Coeur d'Alene.

(Second following page, below) A rustic cabin overlooks Bonner County's Pend Oreille Lake.

(Third following page) Pine-covered hillsides rise steeply from the shores of Upper Priest Lake.

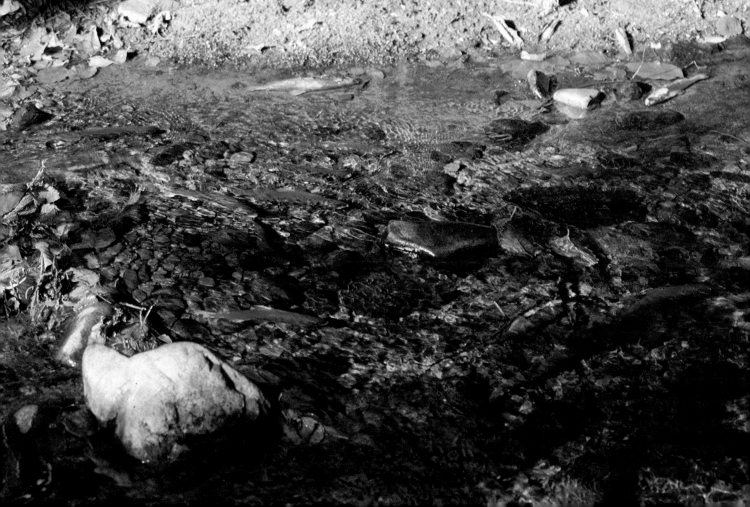

(Preceding page, above) Wind-driven snow clings to the pines, giving them a ghostly aspect in this scene on Roundup Mountain in the Selkirk Range.

(Preceding page, below) Silver salmon spawn in Trestle Creek, Bonner County, in autumn.

(Left) Sunflowers are grown commercially in parts of North Idaho.

(Below) Domestic and wildflowers line the shores of Hayden Lake at the Hayden Lake Country Club.

(Opposite) Like most North Idaho rivers, the Coeur d'Alene flows a rugged and rocky course.

(Following page) A gentle breeze barely ripples the surface of Two Mouth Lake, in Boundary County.

THE WATERY COUNTRY, PLUS ONE

Bonner County is well provided with water, to put it mildly. There's Pend Oreille, one of the country's biggest freshwater lakes; Priest Lake, narrow but long; and many small lakes hidden in the folds of the mountains and hills. The part above water is as dramatic as the lakes themselves. Three great mountain ranges dominate the land. The lofty Selkirks invade it from Boundary County and Canada; the wild mysterious Cabinet Mountains occupy the eastern portion, along with the Bitterroots.

In all, the real estate under water amounts to 110,000 acres and that above it to 1,109,000 acres. A big county. It has one big town—Sandpoint—and a cluster of little ones, mostly hugging the route of the north-south highway which cuts through its middle. It has some history to remember, and because it's a young country, there are still people living who helped make it. It's lumber country, like Kootenai and the other North Idaho counties. Big Pend Oreille Lake did its share of transporting logs in earlier days, and its steamboats were the tug type instead of the sternwheelers common to Coeur d' Alene.

Hope, camped on the toenails of the Cabinet Mountains by the northern shore of Pend Oreille, can still recall some of the earliest days of steamboating hereabouts. The first steamer is still remembered. It was 108 feet long and made out of whip-sawed lumber, meaning lumber cut by two muscular loggers on the ends of a rip saw, one man below and one above the log. The Kootenai and Kalispell Indians of North Idaho were pretty good boat builders, too. Their craft, called ''Kootenai canoes,'' were sturgeon nosed with a downswept prow, and therefore not used on big lakes like Pend Oreille, where waves could easily swamp them. They were river boats, entirely.

Paul Croy, one of the real old-timers in Hope, is something of a legend all by himself. He's been a mule-skinner for the forest service, a teacher of English in a little north woods schoolhouse, and a poet-philosopher whose works have been published. Among his pleasant memories are youthful trips from Hope to Samuels through the woods north of the big lake. In 1910, he remembers, the big first-growth trees were still there. Tall, majestic cedars and huge firs, lining the way like a natural canopy, a cathedral of the living forest. The big lake, he recalls, did logging duty in the winter, too. When Pend Oreille was iced in, horses hauled logs on sleds from Bottle Bay to Kootenai, where the sawmill was. Mail went by boat then, as it still does on North Idaho's two biggest lakes.

(Preceding page, above) Placid waters of the St. Joe River hug the green banks near Calder.
(Preceding page, below) Cataldo Mission is the oldest building in Idaho.

Strangely, the Pend Oreille area is so wild it has restricted invasion by both men and animals over the years. The Indians were discouraged from staying here because of the very dense forest covering, the harsh winters, and the lack of salt deposits. And the hunting was not very productive because lack of browse kept out deer and other grazing animals. In the very early days of settlement, a good deal of mining activity went on around the lake area.

Paul Croy remembers, too, when the ''Pend Oreille route'' was called into service in the wintertime. The Mullan Road from Walla Walla over the Bitterroots through Montana to Missouri was usually snowed in then, and an alternate means of travel had to be taken. So passenger boats from Pend Oreille City at Buttonhook Bay transported people and freight down Pend Oreille Lake to the mouth of Clark Fork River and over Cabinet Gorge into Montana. Today such a journey would not be possible—the Cabinet Gorge Dam on the Clark Fork would be the end of the line. Before the dam was built (in 1952) the river was a wild, rushing stream of spectacular power, cutting its canyon down through the Bitterroot Mountains as it flowed out of Montana toward Pend Oreille. The river's personality is somewhat altered today by the dam, but it is still a mighty stream. Steep and rugged Cabinet Gorge stands as evidence of its past career.

Tales of the north woods are still told in Hope and other towns where early logging is remembered. One of Paul Croy's favorites is about the mail-order bride who came to Hope and promptly set about ''reforming'' her new husband, cleaning up both him and his house to such an extent that he finally moved out in disgust. But this didn't discourage or dislodge the now unwelcome lady. She stayed in the cabin—his cabin. To get rid of her for good and all, he stole up on the roof one night and plugged the chimney. His efforts must have been faulty, because she refused to be smoked out. So he tried again, this time making sure the chimney was good and tight. His second attempt was successful. The unwilling groom was ''cured'' of his mail-order bride, who vanished in a puff of smoke, so to speak.

Although his name seems to have been more-or-less lost in the historical shuffle, David Thompson, the British and Canadian fur trader and explorer, was very important in opening up the Pend Oreille area for settlement. He is very probably the first white man to visit the lake, and in 1809 he built Kullyspell House near present-day East Hope, as a trading post for the Northwest Fur Company and a shelter for his men. Thompson, one of the most skilled geographers who ever lived, is responsible for the first map of Pend Oreille Lake and the surrounding area, which he explored in detail. A memorial near Hope marks the site of Kullyspell House, destroyed by fire in 1832. A more recent building, but fondly remembered by Paul Croy and other citizens of Hope, is Highland House, the town's first hotel. It was probably Hope's first venture into resortery, built specifically for recreationists of the hunting and fishing persuasion. Croy went to first grade there when it was turned into a schoolhouse.

Indian names usually express concepts, and they express them in letter combinations that manage to befuddle most non-Indians when they try to pronounce them. A case in point is Seneaquoteen. It sounds something like a terrible-tasting medicine. But it was once the seat

(Left) Clouds sometimes have an ominous appearance over the expanse of Pend Oreille Lake, signalling one of the lake's infamous storms.

of Kootenai County, formed in 1864, long before Bonner. The word means "crossing of the waters." Seneaquoteen today is a protected marshland across the Pend Oreille River from where Laclede is now. The location is noteworthy as the crossing point on the Pend Oreille River for the old Flathead Trail to Bonners Ferry and Canada. The trail is also known as the Wild Horse Trail (the white man's name for it). The early fur traders called the part that went into Montana the "Road to Buffalo," probably for good and sufficient reasons.

All of North Idaho's big lakes have distinct personalities. Pend Oreille and Coeur d'Alene have very little in common other than their wetness and their importance as logging "highways." Priest Lake is really two closely connected bodies of water, Lower Priest Lake and Upper Priest Lake, but is usually referred to in the singular. A narrow neck of water known as The Thorofare joins the two parts. The Thorofare is an experience by itself; its arching cover of trees, most of them deciduous, brings to mind the shadowy St. Joe. Priest is smaller than the other two big Panhandle lakes, and partly for that reason, perhaps, is considered by some to be the most beautiful of all.

The shape and the remoteness of Priest may also influence such judgements. It is long and narrow—about 24 miles long and one to five miles wide, by its shape and perfect blue color resembling a huge sapphire lying deep within densely forested mountains. Seven islands in the lower lake add their special magic. Some of them are good-size, like Kalispell, or tiny, like Papoose and the Twin Islands. Until fairly recent times no paved roads breached the lake's domain, although the hamlet of Coolin on the southern tip has been around for some time. Now State 57 touches its western edge at some spots. Upper Priest still has no roads leading to it, and so retains much of its status as a complete wilderness, where man and the animals are all short-term visitors. A narrow protective band has been set aside around it as a scenic area.

Marinas at Coolin and Priest River and boat-launching facilities at some other resorts on the lower lake have helped to attract more and more vacationers into the unsurpassed fishing and hunting country. The road from the town of Priest River to Coolin is paved along its whole length, and offers to those who travel it the always soul-stirring experience of riding under a tunnel of trees. The giant evergreens lining the route touch together high overhead to form a lofty cathedral ceiling, with one of the longest naves on record.

The forest around Priest Lake is in places quite impenetrable, with luxuriant undergrowths of ferns, wild shrubs, and wildflowers crowding the space between pine, fir and spruce stands. Innumerable small streams dash through the mountain gullies and over the rocks, ending in Priest or in the smaller lakes cut into the surrounding slopes.

The Priest Lake Area, simply because it was for so long one of the least accessible parts of the continent, was chosen as the home away from home by outlaws, people on the run, and just plain loners. Old timers in the area have stories to tell about some of them, about the mystery of their appearance, of their secretive lives, and sometimes of their disappearance. In the local phrase, some of them "got as goofy as a wooden watch." This is big-tree country, and some of the stories deal with logging and loggers, and how rough a life it was.

The forests and meadows around Priest Lake get a lot of snow in the winter. Sometimes eight feet or better. What does a smart resort area do with all that white stuff? Priest Lake holds dog sled races, in February, when the weather is usually milder, on the meadows around Nordman. There are snowmobile races then, too, but the sled dogs draw the larger number of spectators. It is, after all, more fun to root for a canine engine than a gasoline one. Not to be outdone by Pend Oreille and Coeur d'Alene, Priest Lake one day in May rounds up a giant flotilla of big and little boats to parade around the lake, in connection with related events that open the summer tourist season.

Even though Priest Lake is developing, as it should, a year-round resort economy, its people are being careful to preserve the values that have made their pristine treasure a unique and irreplaceable haven for those who are still looking for their Shangri-la. Its beauty has not suffered from the proximity of man, nor has its quiet charm been violated. For those who go there, "doing" loses some of its importance; just being at Priest Lake is sufficient unto itself.

At the very top of the pile of counties stuffed into North Idaho's Panhandle is Boundary. It's quite another world from Bonner just to the south, where lake water seems to be omnipresent. There are some tiny lakes in Boundary, but its waters are more of the river sort. Two swiftwater streams sweep through the eastern side of the county. The big Kootenai River comes in from Montana along the north edge of the Cabinet Mountains and loops around the northeast corner of Idaho into Canada. The little Moyie heads south from Canada through its wild mountain setting. It flashes through a narrow gorge of almost transcendent beauty. The more massive Kootenai takes a longer time to get where it's going. Below Bonners Ferry and all the way to Canada it slows down and for about 70 miles becomes a gentle waterway for boating. The Kootenai has another distinction; it is the home of the sturgeon, that monster fish that attains 200 pounds and more. The only other Idaho river where they can be caught is the Snake.

Bonners Ferry. Most everyone knows that a man named Bonner got a license (in 1864) to operate a ferry on the Kootenai at the spot where the town was afterward established. Bonners Ferry merits attention as a very good-looking town in its own right and as the centerpiece of a most extravagantly beautiful part of North Idaho. Nearby on US 2/95 are the nonpareil Moyie River Canyon and the Kootenai Canyon. It seems quite fitting that in North Idaho, where the scenic masterpieces seem to vie with one another for first place in the hierarchy of visual splendor, the most perfect, perhaps, of all the creations of wild nature have been saved for the land at the very pinnacle.

(Following pages) Tall, straight pines and lush greenery characterize Bonner County's Moose Lake.

THE SILVER HILLS

The gold was only skin deep. It was what brought A. J. Prichard and the countless hordes who followed him to the North Idaho Mountains. But it wasn't what made Idaho's Shoshone County one of the world's most fabulous repositories of precious minerals, no disrespect to gold intended. What really counted in the context of the national economy was a little deeper and a lot more available—silver and lead. The mineral wealth extracted from the mountains of Shoshone County has exceeded three billion dollars in value since the discovery of the mines in 1885.

That's a lot of bucks, but perhaps only a hint of what is yet to come. But the extractive industries these days are caught in a dilemma. What they are doing represents both a promise and a problem. The wealth of the earth is there for the resourceful to extract it, but the extraction of it doesn't occur without penalties to pay. In the processing of mineral ores, pollution of air and water is an inevitable byproduct. But the Idaho mining industry is facing up to these problems and going a long way toward correcting them.

The mining riches of North Idaho have proved to be far more extensive than most of the other lodes discovered in the West and Southwest in the last century. The lodes beneath the Coeur d'Alenes have really only been tapped, even though they have yielded up billions of dollars worth of silver, lead, and zinc ores. The Silver Valley, as the mining region likes to call itself, was created out of perseverance, struggle, and violence. The famous towns of Kellogg and Wallace were creatures of the rush to the mines, named for the men who were actively associated with the early mining frenzy. Some of the first gold towns, like Eagle and Murray, exploded into existence in the 1880s, then quickly faded after a few frantic years of life. Today they are relics of those incredible storybook days when the news of the Idaho El Dorado first enslaved the imaginations of men.

The call of gold even imperiled the completion of the Mullan Road, built by the military through the Idaho Panhandle in 1859-60, and connecting Fort Benton, at the headwaters of the Missouri River in Montana, with Walla Walla, Washington. Captain John Mullan was in charge of the project, carried out by the Army to provide a quick route through the Northwest territories in case of emergency. The road was completed on schedule, but Mullan had doubts about how long his pickup crew of sometime-prospectors would continue to swing a pick and shovel for a dollar a day when gold-bearing quartz was sticking out all around them in the rugged hills and ravines of the Coeur d'Alenes. He had a real scare one day when a mountain man showed up and offered to pay for some provisions with a nugget of rough gold he had found in a creek bed back in the woods.

The road builders were encamped a few miles from the head of the lake in a Cedar Creek canyon when they held a Fourth of July celebration, raising an American flag to the top of a tall white pine tree. Apparently they made a lot of racket, too, shooting off guns and exploding whatever else was available. The Indians in the vicinity thought the crazy white men were having a war among themselves and rushed to Cataldo Mission to inform the Catholic fathers of the bloody battle. The canyon is now of course a landmark in the Coeur d'Alene area and the flag raising memorialized by establishment of the Mullan Tree Historic Site.

Shoshone County (named for the Shoshone Indians of southern Idaho) is a lot more than mine structures and tailings ponds. The same jumble of rugged mountains that harbor the fabulous mineral lodes also represent some of North Idaho's finest wilderness. While the immediate areas of the mines are no things of beauty the forested hills that surround them indeed are. The monstrous 1910 forest fire left devastation that is still obvious in scarred hillsides, but much replanting has been done, some by the mine operators, so that the scars are gradually receding.

US 10 (Interstate 90) huffs and puffs over and through this interesting country, so that auto tourists can easily pass through the Panhandle without realizing what they're missing. The thing to do is leave the interstate and visit the chief mining towns of Kellogg and Wallace. Wallace, the county seat, fell victim to the aforementioned fire, but has since been rebuilt, part of it climbing up a mountainside. The forest flora are exceptionally varied and beautiful, with wild huckleberries coloring the mountain slopes in late summer down to the Coeur d'Alene South Fork. Even though the area has suffered severe physical injury at the hands of both man and nature, it retains its wild beauty. It's an exceptional place to live and to visit. With continued concern for careful utilization of its resources it will one day, soon, again be a delicious parcel of wild nature with the power to restore the souls of those who live among its hills and streams.

(Following page, above) Reminiscent of early-day logging, an old steam donkey rusts quietly on Hobo Creek, in the St. Joe National Forest.

(Following page, below) Afternoon sunlight seems to seek out a long, colorful tree on this grassy plain in Farragut State Park. Pend Oreille Lake and Bernard Peak form the background.

CREDITS

This book was published with the encouragement and cooperation of First Federal Savings Association of Coeur d'Alene, Idaho.

Separations by San Diego Color Service, San Diego, California

Lithography by Fremont Litho, Fremont, California

Design by Western Photo Group, Beaverton, Oregon

(Preceding page) At Post Falls the river thunders through a narrow, straight-walled gorge of stone.

(Second following page) The Coeur d'Alene River alternates peaceful stretches like this one with rugged, whitewater rapids.

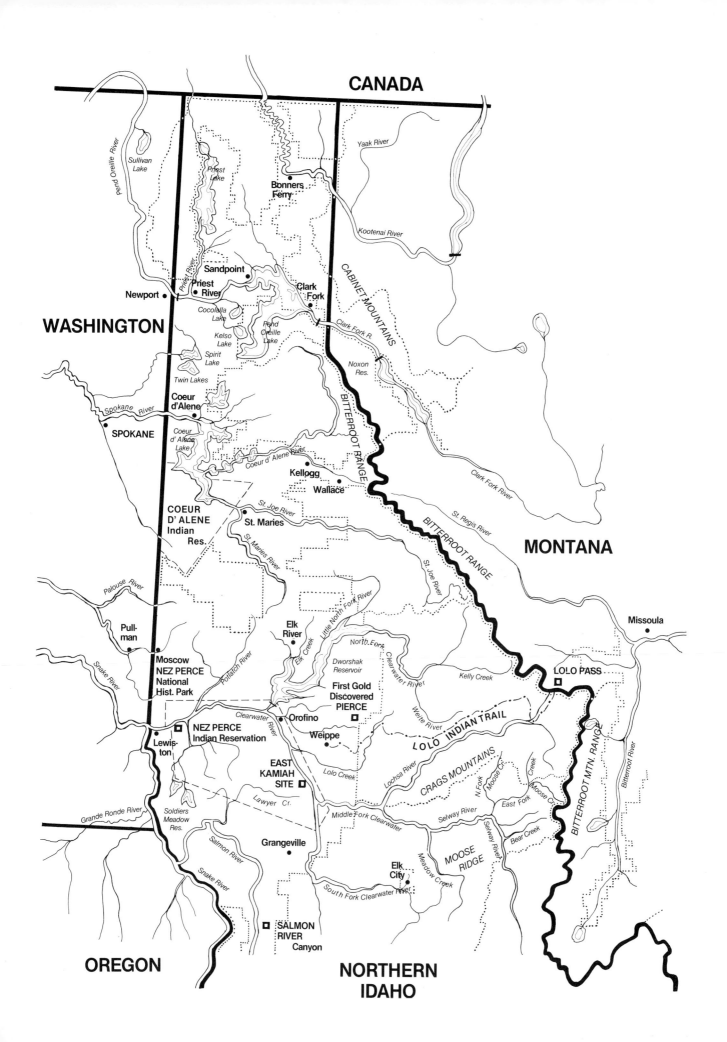